21st Century
Basic Skills
Library

# WHAT DO ANIMALS DO IN FALL?

by Rebecca Felix

Cherry Lake Publishing • Ann Arbor, Michigan

1

CHERRY
LAKE
Publishing

Published in the United States of America
by Cherry Lake Publishing
Ann Arbor, Michigan
www.cherrylakepublishing.com

Consultant: Marla Conn, Read-Ability

Photo Credits: Jin Young Lee/Shutterstock Images, Cover, Title; David P. Lewis/Shutterstock Images, 4, 14; Lijuan Guo/Shutterstock Images, 6; Dmitry Deshevykh/iStockphoto, 8; Celso Pupo/Shutterstock Images, 10; Ron Sanford/iStockphoto, 12; Mike Bauer/Shutterstock Images, 16; Dennis Donohue/Shutterstock Images, 18; Angela Brown/iStockphoto, 20

Library of Congress Cataloging-in-Publication Data
Felix, Rebecca, 1984-
  What do animals do in fall? / Rebecca Felix.
      pages cm. -- (Let's look at fall)
  Audience: 5-7.
  Audience: K to grade 3.
  Includes index.
  ISBN 978-1-61080-907-8 (hardback : alk. paper) -- ISBN 978-1-61080-932-0 (paperback : alk. paper) -- ISBN 978-1-61080-957-3 (ebook) -- ISBN 978-1-61080-982-5 (hosted ebook)
  1.  Animal behavior--Juvenile literature. 2.  Autumn--Juvenile literature. I. Title.

QL751.5.F45 2013
591.5--dc23

                                                      2012030460

Cherry Lake Publishing would like to acknowledge the work of The Partnership for 21st Century Skills.
Please visit www.21stcenturyskills.org for more information.

Printed in the United States of America
Corporate Graphics Inc.
January 2013
CLFA10

# TABLE OF CONTENTS

# Fall Begins

Fall begins after summer. Days get colder. Animals **prepare** for winter.

# Winter Coats

Deer grow **thick** coats to keep warm.

Arctic fox fur turns white. This helps them hide in snow.

## What Do You See?

What do squirrels eat?

# Food for Winter

Squirrels and chipmunks **store** food for winter.

## What Do You See?

What did the bear catch?

Black bears eat a lot. They build up fat. They live off fat in winter.

# Hibernating

Woodchucks prepare to **hibernate**. They fall into a deep winter sleep.

## What Do You See?

What color leaves do you see?

Box turtles hibernate, too. They find winter homes in fall.

# Migrating

Canada geese **migrate**. They fly where it is warmer.

Caribou migrate to find food.
Snow will fall soon!

# Find Out More

## BOOK

Rustad, Martha E. H. *Animals in Fall: Preparing for Winter.*
  Minneapolis: Millbrook Press, Lerner Publications, 2011.

## WEB SITE

**Creature Feature—National Geographic Kids**
*kids.nationalgeographic.com/kids/animals/creaturefeature*
Learn about all kinds of animals.

# Glossary

**hibernate** (HYE-bur-nate) to go into a deep, long sleep
  during winter

**migrate** (MYE-grate) to move to another place

**prepare** (prih-PAIR) to get ready

**store** (STOR) to put something away for later

**thick** (THIK) wide and packed close together

# Home and School Connection

Use this list of words from the book to help your child become a better reader. Word games and writing activities can help beginning readers reinforce literacy skills.

| | | | |
|---|---|---|---|
| animals | deep | grow | squirrels |
| arctic | deer | hibernate | store |
| bears | eat | hide | summer |
| build | fall | homes | thick |
| Canada | fat | leaves | turns |
| caribou | fly | live | turtles |
| chipmunks | food | migrate | warm |
| coats | fox | prepare | white |
| colder | fur | sleep | winter |
| color | geese | snow | woodchucks |

## What Do You See?

...e? is a feature paired with select photos in this book. ...oung readers to interact with visual images in order to ...to integrate content in various media formats.

...ur child further evaluate photos in this book with ...ies. Look at the images in the book without the What ...ture. Ask your child to describe one detail in each ...a color, time of day, animal, or setting.

# Index

# About the Author

Rebecca Felix is an editor and writer. She lives in Minnesota. Deer, geese, and squirrels live in Minnesota, too! Rebecca likes seeing geese fly south in fall.